How Things Happen in the Natural World

by Rachel Sparks Linfield

D1549240

Contents

Longman

Edinburgh Gate
Harlow, Essex

Floating, Freezing and Melting – Icebergs

What are icebergs?

Icebergs are lumps of frozen, fresh water. They are found in the seas near the North and South Poles. These seas are very cold.

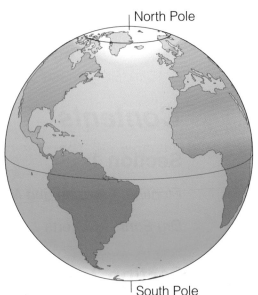
North Pole

South Pole

How are icebergs made?

Icebergs can be made when chunks of ice break from **glaciers**. Glaciers are rivers of ice.

1 Snow falls at the top of a very cold mountain and turns to ice.

2 The ice becomes very heavy. It starts to move down the mountain. This moving river of ice is a glacier.

3 The glacier reaches the sea. Chunks of ice break off and float. These are icebergs.

A thick layer of ice covers much of the North Pole. It is called an **ice sheet**. Around the South Pole is an even thicker sheet of ice. When pieces of ice break from the ice sheets they also make icebergs.

Why are icebergs not salty?

Sea water is salty. When it freezes it is only the watery part that becomes an iceberg. If we melted an iceberg we would have fresh water.

Why are icebergs dangerous?

When ice floats most of it is under the water. This means that most of an iceberg in the sea cannot be seen. For ships this can be very dangerous. The *Titanic* was a famous ship which people thought would be unsinkable. Tragically, on its first trip it crashed into an iceberg and sank.

Icy Disaster

15th April 1912

Last night the Titanic hit an iceberg. Within two hours the great ship had sunk. Over 1,500 people died. Some people drowned whilst others froze in the icy water. Only 705 passengers have been rescued. Survivors say there were not enough lifeboats for all the people on the boat. Relatives of those who have died cannot believe that the Titanic is now at the bottom of the sea. It was supposed to be unsinkable!

How to make home-made icebergs

You will need

- a large plastic tub filled with water
- a freezer
- a large washing-up bowl or plastic fish tank half full of water.

What to do

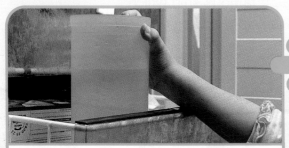

1 Place the plastic tub of water in a freezer and leave it overnight.

2 The next day place the tub in warm water for a few minutes. This will start the iceberg melting and help it to come out of the tub.

3 Now place the iceberg in the tank of water.

Things to investigate

- how much of the iceberg is under the water
- the patterns in the ice as it melts
- how long the iceberg takes to melt
- what happens to the iceberg if it is put in a tank of warm water.

Real icebergs in the sea can take many years to melt. The part which is under the water takes longer to melt than the part which is not in water. The part out of water is blown by the wind and warmed by the Sun. This helps it to melt.

Iceberg record breakers

The tallest iceberg ever recorded was found near Greenland. It was 167 m high. This is just over half the height of the Eiffel Tower.

The largest iceberg recorded was 97 km wide and 335 km long. It was larger than Belgium.

What lives on icebergs?

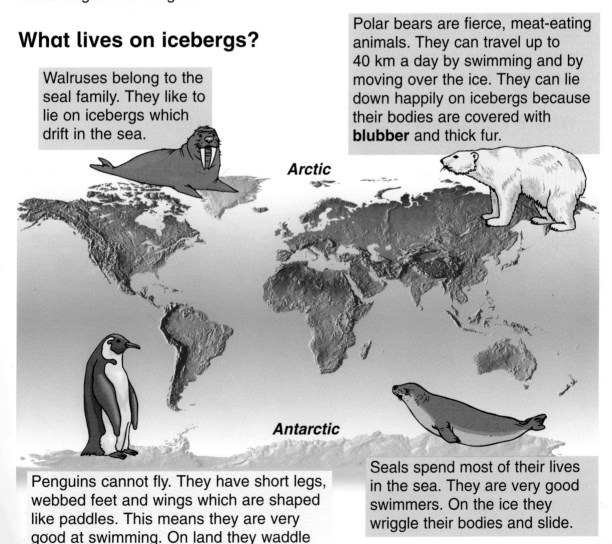

Walruses belong to the seal family. They like to lie on icebergs which drift in the sea.

Polar bears are fierce, meat-eating animals. They can travel up to 40 km a day by swimming and by moving over the ice. They can lie down happily on icebergs because their bodies are covered with **blubber** and thick fur.

Arctic

Antarctic

Penguins cannot fly. They have short legs, webbed feet and wings which are shaped like paddles. This means they are very good at swimming. On land they waddle on their feet or slide on their chests.

Seals spend most of their lives in the sea. They are very good swimmers. On the ice they wriggle their bodies and slide.

Dry Earth – Deserts

What is a desert?

Deserts are places where it is dry nearly all the time. This photograph shows the Sahara Desert which is in Africa. It is the largest desert in the world.

The Sahara Desert is very sandy. Not all deserts are made from sand. Some deserts are made from rocks, pebbles and gravel. The North and South Poles are icy deserts. Here snow does not often fall and little water soaks into the ground. This chapter will look at the sandy and stony deserts.

Where can deserts be found in the world?

About one fifth of the land in the world is desert land. This map shows where there are deserts.

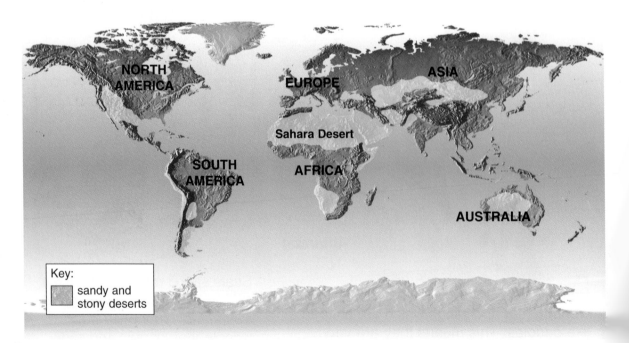

NORTH AMERICA

EUROPE

ASIA

Sahara Desert

SOUTH AMERICA

AFRICA

AUSTRALIA

Key:
sandy and stony deserts

Where did the sand in the sandy deserts come from?

It takes thousands of years to make sand. Sand is made from rock that has been worn away into tiny grains. This happens when rocks are battered by the weather. As well as helping to turn rocks into sand, wind helps to make and change the scenery. The wind makes sand dunes.

How are sand dunes made?

A sand dune is a hill of sand. There are many dunes in the Sahara Desert.

Dunes are usually made around a rock or a plant. This flow chart shows what happens.

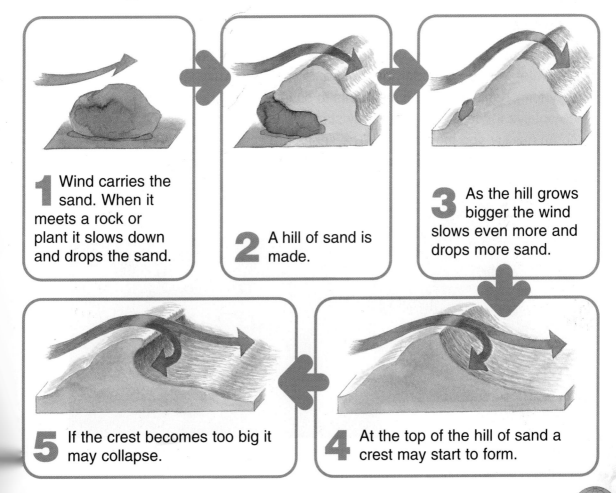

1 Wind carries the sand. When it meets a rock or plant it slows down and drops the sand.

2 A hill of sand is made.

3 As the hill grows bigger the wind slows even more and drops more sand.

5 If the crest becomes too big it may collapse.

4 At the top of the hill of sand a crest may start to form.

How can plants and animals survive in a desert?

Living things need water to survive. Yet less than 25 cm of rain falls each year in a desert. This is not very much water. The next time it rains make a **rain gauge** and put it outside to collect rain water. See how long it takes you to collect as much water as a desert would have in a year!

Plants and animals which can survive in deserts have special features which help them to find and/or save water.

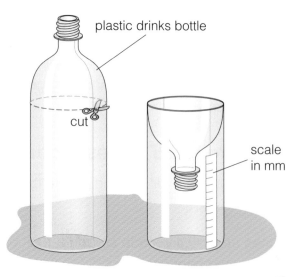

plastic drinks bottle

cut

scale in mm

Desert plants

Some desert plants have very long roots. These roots help the plants to get water from deep under the ground. Some have waxy leaves and very thick bark. This helps the plants to save water. Other desert plants do not live for very long. They only start to grow when it rains. Flowers come quickly and make seeds. The seeds are scattered before the plants die. The seeds then wait for the next rain to come before they send out shoots and flower. This may not be for many years.

Dune primrose

Cardon cactus

Cactus plants grow in the deserts in America. They often have roots that spread out to find as much water as possible.

Desert animals

Some *insects* which live in the desert have bodies with hard, waxy outer coverings, which help to conserve moisture. When it is too hot they shelter in tiny holes in rocks.

Darkling Beetle

The *Gila Monster* is a poisonous lizard. It has a very thick tail which can store fat. When there is little food in the desert it can use this fat for energy. Its scaly skin helps it to save water.

Gila Monster

Rattlesnake

Rattlesnakes have loose rings of skin at the ends of their tails. They rattle these rings to scare enemies. In the desert it is more sensible to rattle a tail than to hiss since hissing would use water.

Birds in the deserts are lucky because they can fly to search for water. Meat-eating birds like the Harris hawk do not need to find water for drinking. Instead they get their **moisture** from the animals they catch and eat.

Harris Hawk

9

Camels have many features which help them to survive without food or water in the desert for many days.

The hump stores fat. This can be used for energy. The hump shrinks as the fat is used.

Long eyelashes help to protect the eyes from sand and the Sun.

The nostrils can be closed if there is a sand storm.

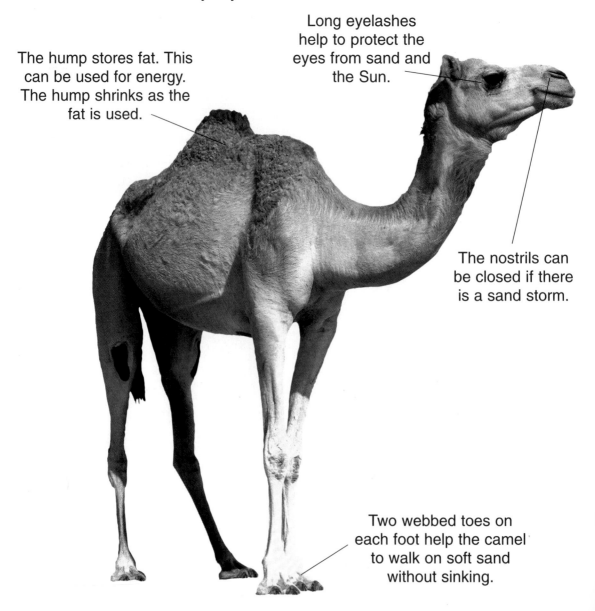

Two webbed toes on each foot help the camel to walk on soft sand without sinking.

Many of the deserts in the world are growing. This is happening partly because land on the edge of the deserts is being misused by people. **Vegetation** has been cut down and burnt. Farmers have used some land so much that animals cannot graze on it anymore. Desert plants act as barriers to desert sand. When animals eat these plants, the desert starts to spread.

Spinning Winds –
Hurricanes and Tornadoes

What is a hurricane?

Hurricanes are mighty storms with fierce, swirling winds. They begin in the Tropics, the area which is just north and south of the **Equator**. Here the Earth is very hot and so are the oceans. Hurricanes start over warm, tropical oceans which have temperatures above 27 °C. They often travel at speeds of over 120 km per hour and measure more than 400 km in **diameter**. They can create huge waves and bring heavy rain. Once hurricanes reach land they can cause much damage to buildings, trees, cars and anything which lies in their way. The rain and waves can also cause flooding.

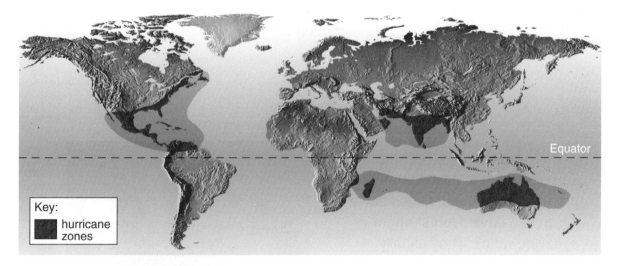

Equator

Key:
hurricane zones

How are hurricanes formed?

Hurricanes are formed when **water vapour** rising from the sea makes a thick bank of cloud. As the warm vapour and the air rise they begin to spin, making an upward spiral. More air then rushes in underneath and so the spiralling continues and makes a hurricane. At the centre of each hurricane is the **eye**. This is a calm, cloudless area around which the violent winds spin. Hurricanes which happen north of the Equator turn in an anti-clockwise direction. Those which happen south of the Equator spin in a clockwise direction.

How are hurricanes recorded?

In the 19th century an Australian man named Clement Wraggle gave hurricanes the names of people he had quarrelled with. Today the World Meteorological Organisation gives hurricanes names so that they can be identified and recorded. Each year they begin with the letter A and then go through the alphabet choosing first a male and then a female name. In 1998 the names Alex, Bonnie, Charley, Danielle and Earl were given to five Atlantic hurricanes.

The **Saffir–Simpson Scale** is used to describe the damage which a hurricane does. It classifies hurricanes on a scale of 1 to 5 where 5 is the worst level of damage.

Saffir–Simpson category	Damage caused
1	minimal
2	moderate
3	extensive
4	extreme
5	catastrophic

What is a tornado?

Tornadoes are violent storms that are smaller than hurricanes but which can have even stronger spiralling winds. They usually measure about 100 m in diameter. They begin in big thunderclouds. Fast winds which pass over the clouds cause rising warm air within the clouds to spin. As the spinning becomes faster and stronger a tornado is formed. Tornadoes can suck up cars and even buildings.

The **Fujita Scale** describes the wind speed and the damage that a tornado can do.

Fujita category	Level of damage	Wind speed in km/hour
F–0	light	up to 116
F–1	moderate	117–180
F–2	considerable	181–253
F–3	severe	254–332
F–4	devastating	333–419
F–5	incredible	420+

How to make a bottle tornado

You will need

- water
- a small, clear, plastic bottle
- washing-up liquid.

What to do

1 Almost fill the bottle with water.

2 Add a few drops of washing up liquid and gently swirl the bottle so the liquid and water mix together but do not cause too many soap bubbles. Screw the lid on tightly.

3 Hold the bottle upside down around the neck. Vigorously swirl the bottle in one direction and then stop. If the bottle has been rotated quickly enough a small tornado will be seen in the centre of the bottle.

What have famous hurricanes and tornadoes done?

Hurricanes and tornadoes can cause a great deal of damage. Many people have lost their homes and all their possessions through being caught up in these dreadful spiralling storms. Many people have also been killed. Newspapers throughout the world often record the progress of tornadoes and hurricanes, and the problems they cause.

October 1998

Hurricane Mitch which began as a Caribbean tropical storm has now caused wide devastation. The hurricane has led to terrible flooding in Honduras and the capital has been ruined. In Nicaragua mud slides have killed over 1200 people.

September 1999

Over two million Americans have left their homes to try and escape from Hurricane Floyd. In pouring rain thousands of cars crawled along freeways trying to flee from the coast. This was the largest evacuation in American history.

Sometimes hurricanes and tornadoes lead to strange events. In the United States of America a railway engine was picked up by a tornado. Whilst in the air it was turned around and then put back on a nearby rail track going in the opposite direction! In 1940 a tornado in Nizhniy Novgorod, Russia uncovered an ancient treasure chest. It picked the chest up and then sprinkled coins over the village. Over 1000 coins were collected.

Turning to Stone – Fossils

What are fossils?

Fossils are the stony remains or **evidence** of animals and plants that died millions of years ago. Fossils show us that there was life on Earth at least 3500 million years ago. They also provide some information about the kinds of creatures and plants that were alive. This time line shows some of the facts that have been discovered through studying fossils.

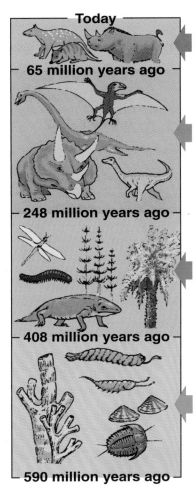

Today

65 million years ago

248 million years ago

408 million years ago

590 million years ago

Cenozoic World
• plants and animals alive similar to those we have today

Mesozoic World
• dinosaurs alive
• flowering plants appeared

Late Palaeozoic World
• many **amphibians, reptiles** and insects on land eating vegetation

Early Palaeozoic World
• many animals without backbones alive
• much life in the sea
• plants beginning to live on the land

How are fossils made?

It takes millions of years for fossils to be made. Plants and animals begin to rot as soon as they die, so in order for a fossil to be made the plant or animal must be buried quickly. Burying plants and animals helps to preserve the hard parts such as the teeth, bones and shells. Over millions of years the mud and sand that has mixed with these parts harden into rock. If water leaks into the rock the animal and plant remains may dissolve leaving a **fossil mould**. **Minerals** can then fill the mould. This is one of the ways in which fossils are formed.

How to make a plaster of Paris fossil

You will need

- plaster of Paris
- plasticine
- petroleum jelly
- a paper clip
- a hard natural object such as a shell or a leaf with distinct veins
- a strip of card about 30 cm × 8 cm
- a plastic tray.

What to do

1 Flatten the plasticine ball into a disk shape which is about 4 cm thick and has a diameter slightly larger than the natural object.

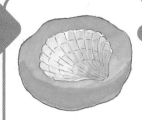

2 Press the object on the plasticine so that a clear print of it is formed.

3 Cover the plasticine print with a thin layer of petroleum jelly. This will stop the plaster of Paris from sticking too tightly to the plasticine.

5 Place the fossil mould in the plastic tray. Fill the mould with plaster of Paris and leave it to set. When it is set remove the card strip and plasticine. You will be left with a plaster of Paris fossil of your natural object.

4 Wind the card strip around the plasticine tightly to make a cylinder and fasten it with a paper clip. Smear petroleum jelly around the inside of the card.

What has been fossilised?

Although we can learn a lot about the history of our Earth from studying fossils, there are still many things we do not know about the animals and plants that lived millions of years ago. One problem is that only a small number of the types of plants and creatures that were alive have been preserved as fossils. For example, fossils of animals with soft bodies such as worms are very rare. Also, because it is usually the hard parts of animals that are **fossilised** we are unable to tell much about the animals' colours, sizes or whether they had fur. Footprints and animal trails have been fossilised. The prints are useful for learning about the shape and size of animal feet but it is hard to tell much about the number of animals because one animal can make many footprints! Nevertheless, there are many wonderful fossils that can give us a glimpse of what life was like. It is also fascinating to discover from fossils that some of the plants and creatures alive today are very similar to ones that were alive so very long ago.

Brittle starfish

Ammonite

Lizard skeleton

Fern

Sea urchin

Erupting Earth – Volcanoes

What is a volcano?

A volcano is an opening in the Earth's surface through which molten rock and gas from deep inside the Earth can escape. The mountains that form when **magma**, the molten rock, is released are also known as volcanoes. The magma which comes out of the volcano is called **lava**.

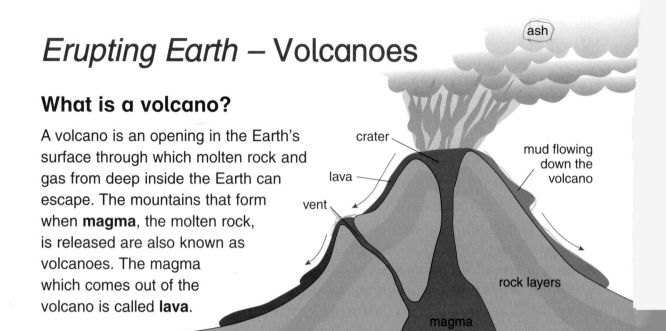

Where do volcanoes most often occur?

The Earth is made up of three layers. At the centre is the **core**, a ball of extremely hot metal. People believe that the core is solid on the inside and liquid on the outside. The **mantle** surrounds the core. It is made from rock and is so hot that parts of the mantle flow like treacle. The outer layer of the Earth is called the **crust** and is made from rocks.

The crust is not one solid piece but is split into about fifteen large bits called **plates**. Each plate is about the size of an ocean or continent. The plates float on top of the mantle because the rock from which they are made is less dense than the mantle. **Oceanic plates** are ones that are covered by oceans. **Continental plates** carry the continents. Some plates have both sea and land on them.

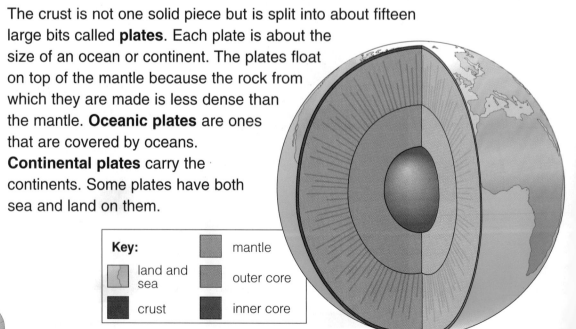

Key:

land and sea

crust

mantle

outer core

inner core

Volcanoes are often found where two plates meet. Here magma can find a way through cracks in the Earth's crust. The boundaries between plates are known as **plate margins**.

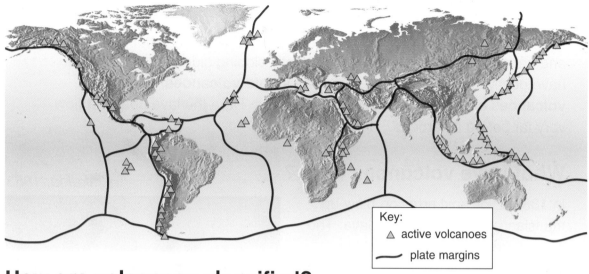

Key:
△ active volcanoes
⌒ plate margins

How are volcanoes classified?

Volcanoes are initially classified as **extinct**, **dormant** or **active** according to whether they are likely or unlikely to erupt.

Extinct volcanoes are ones that have shown no signs of activity for thousands of years. Edinburgh Castle in Scotland sits on a volcano that has been extinct for 325 million years.

Extinct volcanoes can sometimes take us by surprise. In 1973, Helgafell, a volcano in Iceland that was considered extinct, erupted. Many homes were buried and burnt by the red hot lava.

Dormant volcanoes are ones that are said to be sleeping but which could erupt again. Mount Fujiyama in Japan is a dormant volcano. It has not erupted since 1707 but has lava simmering in the **crater** and rising steam.

Active volcanoes are ones that still erupt. There are about 500 active volcanoes in the world and about 30 erupt each year.

Volcanoes come in a variety of sizes and shapes depending upon the amount and temperature of the lava which they create and the force with which it comes out of the Earth. If lava travels a long way before it cools and hardens, it forms a volcano with gently sloping sides. Volcanoes that have gently sloping sides are known as **shield volcanoes**. **Strato volcanoes** are cone-shaped with steep sides. Here the lava does not flow very far before it hardens.

What have volcanoes done?

Krakatoa, 1883

In 1883 a volcanic eruption blew up the island of Krakatoa near Java. The noise from the explosion could be heard in Australia, 4800 km away. Volcanic dust carried by the wind caused brilliant sunsets that could be seen even in London, England. The volcano caused gigantic waves called **tsunamis** that crashed on Sumatra and Java and killed 36 000 people.

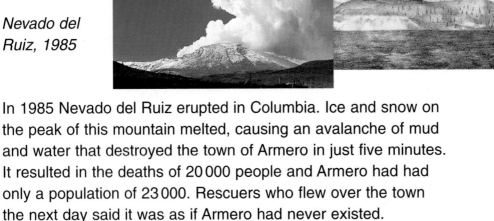

Nevado del Ruiz, 1985

In 1985 Nevado del Ruiz erupted in Columbia. Ice and snow on the peak of this mountain melted, causing an avalanche of mud and water that destroyed the town of Armero in just five minutes. It resulted in the deaths of 20 000 people and Armero had had only a population of 23 000. Rescuers who flew over the town the next day said it was as if Armero had never existed.

How to make an erupting volcano

You will need

- a large, deep sided, plastic bowl
- vinegar
- red food colouring.
- sand and stones
- bicarbonate of soda

You should do this with an adult. Your face should never be near the volcano and especially not when it erupts. Wear safety spectacles. It is important to cover the table on which you are working before you begin.

What to do

1 One quarter fill a small plastic bottle with bicarbonate of soda and place the bottle in the centre of the plastic bowl.

2 Surround the bottle with small stones covered with sand and pat it into a shape like a volcano, making sure the neck of the bottle can be seen.

3 Quickly pour vinegar mixed with red food colouring into the bottle and watch your volcano erupt. It erupts because the vinegar mixes with the bicarbonate of soda to make bubbles of carbon dioxide.

Should people live near active volcanoes?

When a volcano erupts, the nearby land can be covered with volcanic ash. As long as the layer of ash is not too deep it is very good for plants and makes the soil extremely fertile. For example, each year three rice crops can be grown on the slopes of Gunung Agung in Bali. Yet, when this volcano erupted in 1963, 2000 people were killed.

Volcanic rocks are very hot. If they are drilled hot water in the cracks can escape to the Earth's surface and the steam can be used to make electricity. In Iceland there are many hot springs that are used for both heating and hot water.

Many people choose to live by active volcanoes and enjoy the benefits they can bring. Yet these people must also worry about the threat that the volcanoes could erupt at any time. We cannot stop volcanoes from erupting but scientists can help people to live more safely in active regions by predicting when volcanoes might erupt. **Seismometers** can be used to detect volcanic **tremors** and provide early warnings of eruptions.

The city of Pompeii was destroyed when Vesuvius erupted in 79 AD

Shaking Earth – Earthquakes

What is an earthquake?

An earthquake is a vibration in the Earth's **crust**. Every year about eleven million earthquakes happen but fortunately most of them are very small. Every two weeks a large earthquake occurs but luckily the majority take place under the sea where little damage is done. Around 34 000 earthquakes are strong enough to be detected by **seismometers**, the instruments which are used to measure the power of Earth **tremors**.

Why do earthquakes happen?

The Earth's crust is made up of about fifteen large pieces called **plates**. When the plates collide great amounts of energy cause rocks to push against rocks. Sometimes parts of the plates slide gradually over other parts but, in other places, the plates are unable to slide. Over the years these plates continue to push until suddenly they do slip and a lot of energy is released. **Shock waves** are then emitted from this place in all directions. If the waves arrive at the Earth's surface they may be felt as earthquakes. The point underground where the plate movement happened is called the **focus** of the earthquake.

What are shock waves like?

Earthquakes cause two different types of wave. Waves which move on the Earth's surface are called **surface waves**. Those which can travel through rock are called **body waves**. People who predict earthquakes and who measure their size and effect usually receive their first information as a result of **primary waves**, usually known as P waves. These body waves travel like sound waves. A good way to imagine P waves is to stretch a slinky spring along the ground, hold one end still and push the other end. Waves can be seen travelling along the spring as a series of **compressions** and **expansions**. P waves are like this and can travel through solids and liquids.

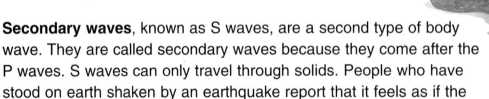

Secondary waves, known as S waves, are a second type of body wave. They are called secondary waves because they come after the P waves. S waves can only travel through solids. People who have stood on earth shaken by an earthquake report that it feels as if the earth is being rippled up and down. This effect is usually caused by S waves. A skipping rope can be used to demonstrate S waves.

There are also two kinds of surface waves, **Love waves** and **Rayleigh waves**. As Love waves travel forwards they push rocks sideways whilst Rayleigh waves move down and up. Surface waves cause more damage to structures on the Earth's surface than body waves because they travel slower than body waves and therefore take longer to pass through.

What are fault lines?

When the Earth's plates move and push against each other or pull apart they can make rocks in the Earth's crust crumple or even crack. These cracks in large blocks of stone are known as **faults** and the lines which the cracks cause are known as **fault lines**. The biggest fault lines in the world happen at the **plate margins**, the places where plates meet. One of the most famous fault lines in the world is the San Andreas Fault, which lies along the Pacific Coast in California in the United States of America. The fault is about 1200 km long and is in one of the world's major earthquake zones.

What damage have massive earthquakes caused?

The most dangerous earthquakes are those which occur between the Earth's crust and 70 km below. They can be so powerful that within a few minutes buildings are shaken to pieces. Fires often break out as gas pipes and electricity cables are damaged and water supplies are cut off.

In 1906 a violent earthquake in San Francisco caused tremendous damage. Many homes and businesses were flattened. Around 700 people died and 250 000 people were made homeless. Following this earthquake, major rebuilding work was necessary. Scientists studying the 1906 earthquake predicted that another major one was likely to happen in San Francisco and, due to the increase in the number of buildings and people living in the city, it was likely to cause even more casualties. On Tuesday 17 October, 1989 at 5.04 pm the earthquake happened. Fortunately, of the three million people in the city only 68 were killed but 3757 were injured, 27 000 businesses were damaged and 1400 homes were destroyed.

San Francisco, 1989

San Francisco, 1906

Kobe, 1995

In 1995 a Japanese earthquake in Kobe killed over 5000 people,
injured 27 000 and made 370 000 homeless. Sadly this disaster was
one which people had thought would never happen. Kobe had been
bombed during World War II and when the city had been rebuilt the
bridges, roads and buildings were said to be earthquake-proof. The
Kobe earthquake encouraged architects all over the world to
consider what had gone wrong and to investigate how to make
buildings and other structures which could survive an earthquake.

How are earthquakes measured?

Two scales are used to measure earthquakes. The **Mercali Scale** describes the effect that an earthquake has on buildings and people.

Mercali Scale	Effect on buildings and people
1–2	It is difficult to feel the vibrations.
3–4	Loose objects move.
5–6	Buildings are damaged slightly. Objects fall.
7–8	Chimneys fall, walls crack and people start to panic.
9–10	Buildings collapse.
11–12	Cracks appear in the ground. Buildings are destroyed.

The **Richter Scale** measures the power of an earthquake's waves. Earthquakes which measure less than 3 on the Richter Scale are scarcely felt. Ones which measure more than 6 cause damage. Any which are more than 8 are devastating.

Richter Scale	Effect on buildings and people
less than 3.4	No noticeable effects.
3.5–4.2	Some people might feel the vibrations.
4.3–4.8	Most people feel the vibrations. Windows rattle.
4.9–5.4	Everyone notices the vibrations. Objects may fall off shelves.
5.5–6.1	Cracks appear in walls.
6.2–6.9	Chimneys fall.
7.0–7.3	Bridges twist, some buildings collapse.
7.4–7.9	Most buildings collapse.
more than 8.0	Total destruction.

The Transamerica Pyramid skyscraper in San Francisco

What can we do to make buildings more earthquake resistant?

- Buildings made from wood on solid ground are less likely to fall down than ones made out of bricks.

- Buildings must be flexible if they are to survive earthquake vibrations. Skyscrapers built on steel frames can sway and so sometimes survive earthquakes without falling down.

- The shape of a building can affect its ability to withstand an earthquake. In San Francisco the tallest building is a pyramid-shaped skyscraper. It was opened in 1972 and had been specially designed to be earthquake-proof.

Glossary

active volcanoes   Volcanoes which still erupt.

amphibian   A cold-blooded animal which can live both on land and in water.

blubber   A layer of fat which helps animals that live in very cold places to keep warm.

body waves   Shock waves that can travel through rock.

compression   A squeeze.

continental plates   Pieces of the Earth's crust which carry continents.

core   The ball-shaped centre layer of the Earth, made of extremely hot metal which is solid on the inside and liquid on the outside.

crater   The hollow at the top of a volcano.

crust   The solid skin around the Earth.

diameter   A line through the centre of a circle.

dormant volcanoes   'Sleeping' volcanoes which are not active but which could erupt again.

Equator   An imaginary line around the middle of the Earth.

evidence   Proof.

expansion   An increase in size.

extinct volcanoes   Volcanoes that have shown no signs of activity for thousands of years.

eye   The calm centre of a hurricane.

fault   Cracks in large blocks of rock on the Earth's crust.

fault lines   The lines caused by cracks in the Earth's crust.

focus   The point of the earthquake where plate movement happened.

fossil mould   Imprint which can be filled with minerals to make a fossil.

fossilise   The preserving of the remains of a plant or animal in rock.

Fujita Scale   Measure of wind speed and damage by a tornado.

glacier	River of ice.
ice sheet	A thick layer of ice.
lava	Molten rock that comes out of a volcano.
Love waves	Surface shock waves that push sideways.
magma	Melted rock.
mantle	The outside of the Earth's core.
Mercali Scale	Measure of the effect of an earthquake on people and buildings.
mineral	A chemical substance which occurs naturally in the Earth.
moisture	Dampness.
oceanic plates	Pieces of the Earth's crust which are covered by oceans.
plates	Pieces of the Earth's crust.
plate margins	Edges of a plate.
primary waves	Body waves that travel as a series of compressions.
rain gauge	An instrument used to measure rainfall.
Rayleigh waves	Surface waves that move up and down.
reptile	A class of animals including snakes, lizards, alligators and turtles.
Richter Scale	Measure of the power of an earthquake's waves.
Saffir-Simpson Scale	Measure of hurricane damage.
secondary waves	Body waves that travel up and down.
seismometer	An instrument used to detect earthquakes and volcanoes.
shield volcanoes	Volcanoes with gently sloping sides.
shock waves	Waves of movement which result from the plates in the Earth's crust slipping suddenly.
strato volcanoes	Cone-shaped volcanoes with steep sides.
surface waves	Shock waves that move on the Earth's surface.
tremor	A vibration or shake.
tsunamis	Huge ocean waves.
vegetation	Plants.
water vapour	A gas form of water.

Index